THE WELSH THREE THOUSANDS
A Guide for Walkers and Fell Runners

Roy Clayton 1993
ISBN 0 9515996 3 1

Photographs:-
Front Cover: Tryfan and Llyn Ogwen from Y Garn
Rear Cover: The view over Cwm Dyli to Crib Goch from Bwlch Glas
All photos by the author except for P18 (old postcard) & P62 (Harvey
Lloyd)

Acknowledgments:
I would like to thank those who have helped me in the publica-
tion of this book. Harvey Lloyd, who has been a major source of
detailed knowledge of the area; my brother James and friends
Anthony Wilson and Kieran Hartley, who have tramped the hills
with me, more often than not in less than perfect conditions;
Ken Vickers for his invaluable advice and John Gillham for his
support and encouragement.

For my children
Ricky and Natasha

THE WELSH THREE THOUSANDS
A Guide for Walkers and Fell Runners

By Roy Clayton

with editorial and historical assistance from Harvey Lloyd
Maps and drawings by John Gillham

Grey Stone Books
Hoddlesden

CITY BLUES

In the city there are no horizons
Man cannot see the boundaries of his soul.
In the city, light and sound fall in pools
They do not spread, escape the murky bowl.

Only in the mountains can you see far enough,
And know enough to understand.
I have seen the sky, and lost it again
I must return to the hills and sanity regain.

C. McColl

The Crib Goch Pinnacles and Yr Wyddfa, the Snowdon's massif's main peak

CONTENTS

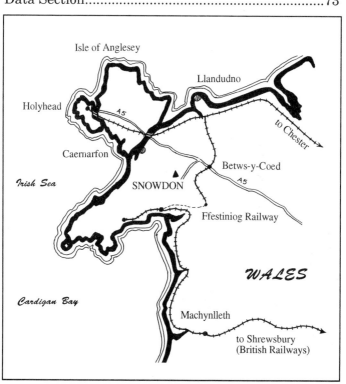

My foreword could begin like a child's story. "Once upon a time there was a man named E.G. Rowland, who liked to walk amongst the Welsh Hills and decided to write a book called *Hill Walking in Snowdonia*....

E.G. Rowland was one of the persons who introduced me to the region nearly forty years ago - forty years that have brought to me the most wonderful experiences. Known even in the fifties as "the old man of the mountains", the written words of this veteran rambler and mountaineer probably became part of the motivation and inspiration leading to the upturn in interest in hill walking in the fifties.

As the Youth Hostel Warden at Pen y Pass I now live amongst these glorious mountains and I was therefore delighted when approached by Roy Clayton to help with the production of this book. In putting it together we hope that it will spread the call of the mountains to a wider public.

My first attempt at the *Welsh Three Thousands* took place on a Sunday in June. At 5 am. I am never at my best and peering into a cloudy environment, crisscrossed with the beams of head-torches was not encouraging for a novice of long mountain treks. I was accompanied by a group of experienced mountain people, however and I had worked at getting fit. It was a case of head down and hope for better weather later in the day. Luck was with us and we came through the cloud on Crib Goch - the cotton wool layer below extending towards Anglesey and the Irish Sea. The sun warmed our cold limbs. Suddenly Snowdon was a wonderful place to be.

The day progressed well. Support groups in Nant Peris and Ogwen supplied much needed sustenance. The traverse of the Carneddau was highlighted by a glorious setting sun, diluting the pain and fatigue that the days rigours had brought about.

The next attempt was quite different. The day again started wet and miserable but the traverse of Crib Goch, Carnedd Ugain and Snowdon passed reasonably well. The trouble started on the descent to Nant Peris. A bad choice of route and laziness in not consulting a compass, brought us to very steep ground above Cwm Glas Bach and delayed our arrival in the village until late morning. The weather continued to deteriorate and morale was low. The Glyders were very wet and the attempt was aborted at Ogwen. We learned from our foolishness. A compass in the rucksack does not help in route finding, even in the hills we thought we knew so well!

Safety in the Mountains

Most readers will not need reminding that mountains are dangerous places and that safety should not be taken for granted. Snowdonia is no place for the unprepared.Before an attempt is made on the Three Thousands a great deal of preparation needs to be undertaken. A good level of fitness is required of everyone. The fitness can be built up by practice days over part of the route, preferably in all types of weather. Someone with prior knowledge of the area is a passport to success. It goes without saying that one should be properly equipped, always erring on the cautious side with regards the weather and what is to be carried. Getting the right balance is difficult,for a light rucksack is important and Murphy's Law says that if you haven't brought it you will need it and if you have it you will not! Comfortable boots, good waterproofs, map, compass and whistle should be supplemented by emergency food rations, a torch and bivvi bag. Make sure that using a map and compass are second nature: taking part in orienteering events is excellent practice once the basic elements are learned. Make sure that someone trustworthy has details of your itinerary and emergency escape routes and ensure that you contact them if delayed or forced to abandon the excursion.

For **fell runners** who wish to attempt the traverse, all the preceding remarks apply. There is definitely no place for the unfit and unprepared. Within the sport of fellrunning there have been several fatalities over the years. The tragedies have often been brought about by a severe deterioration in weather conditions. The most important point to make is that the body needs protection from the elements. Fortunately these days there is a range of waterproof suits that are portable and light. When purchasing make sure that the jackets are large enough and with long sleeves that will pull over the hands. Roomy hoods with self-locking drawcords are advisable. Over-trousers should slip over running shoes. Pockets are useful.

A support team with a car at Nant Peris or Ogwen or both can be very welcome. It can facilitate a change of

Harvey in the mountains of Snowdonia that he knows so well.

clothes and proper refreshment - possibly the difference between success and failure.

Finally a word about conservation of the environment over which we travel.The National Parks are sponsored and managed to promote "quiet enjoyment" for the population. Headlines such as "Charity runners threaten Snowdon" in the media suggest that there is a resistance to any sort of organised event. The land in the Snowdonia National Park is largely privately owned and the route crosses several ecologically sensitive sites - Snowdonia is well known for its rare alpine plants. In addition to this local farmers are finding it increasingly difficult to make a living from rearing sheep on such hostile terrain. The problems have been made worse by the increasing numbers of walkers and it is important that everybody should be concerned to protect this fragile region. Always follow the Country Code and be considerate to other landowners and landusers.

The popularity of the Welsh 3's has been firmly established. The greats will continue to work at knocking minutes off existing records; the also-rans will try to better their previous times and the mountains will always be there for anyone, whether rich or poor - to walk over to run over or simply to admire from the comfort of valley or village.

THE
WELSH THREE THOUSANDS ROUTE

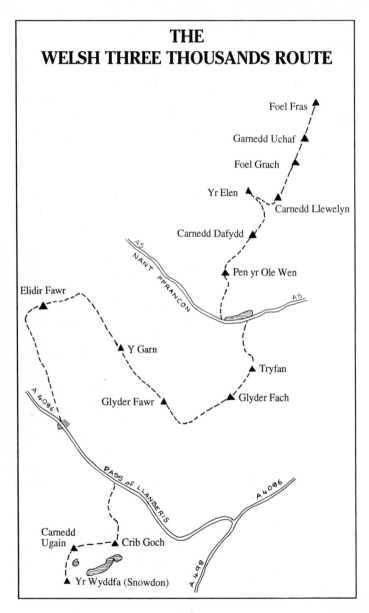

INTRODUCTION

The fifteen Welsh three-thousand foot peaks lie in close proximity within the northern region of the Snowdonia National Park and are all contained in three ranges - the Carneddau, the Glyders (or Glyderau) and Snowdon. Since Thomas Firbank's fascinating account of the Welsh Three Thousands Race in his book 'I Bought a Mountain' it has caught the imagination of a great number of intrepid mountaineers, runners and walkers. It was Firbank who laid down the basic rules which stand today. (i.e. that the race starts on the top of Snowdon, finishes on Foel Fras and that the tops of all the eligible summits must be touched on the way.)

In those days it was accepted that there were fourteen summits with a drop of at least fifty foot in all directions. Since the Ordnance Survey's remeasurement, the Carneddau peak of Garnedd Uchaf has been adjudged to be 3038 feet above sea level and thus has been added to the list. If you adhered to the Scottish 'Munro' rules there would only be eight Welsh Three Thousands. Crib Goch, Carnedd Ugain, Glyder Fach, Pen yr Ole Wen, Yr Elen, Foel Grach and Garnedd Uchaf would all be omitted. Conversely I have heard it said that Castell y Gwynt on Glyder Fach and Clogwyn y Person on Carnedd Ugain would qualify under the fifty foot rule - the mind boggles. Mathematics has no business in the mountains and I do not wish to get bogged down with classification of what constitutes a peak or mountain. Nobody will make me believe Crib Goch is not a true mountain.

Although, in the interests of European Unity, we have gone metric, most mountain walkers demand the retention of the 'foot', for to diminish our noble peaks' altitude to a few hundred metres seems to diminish their very stature. My concession to Maastricht and its method of measurement is to put the "beloved' metre in brackets.

My first acquaintance with Wales was on one of those whistle-stop coach tours. The driver proudly pointed out the peaks of Snowdon, the principality's highest mountain. My senses were more stirred by the rugged ramparts of the Glyder Range, which soar supremely above Ogwen and the Pass of Llanberis. Standing on the shores of Llyn Ogwen, my eyes were rivetted to the intimidating crest of Tryfan. I watched as climbers grappled with the hard rocky buttresses and walkers with brightly coloured cagouls clambered over crags and scree to the skyline. The seeds of my interest in the mountains were sewn.

In June 1977, a couple of years later, I ventured onto the hills as a member of a school-party intent on doing four days of the Pennine Way. Not even the cumbersome pack, which was hoisted onto my back, could subdue my high spirits as we set forth from Malham. Fifty miles later I sat on the return coach aching from head to toe and yearning for a hot bath. I was content in the knowledge that I would never again have to set foot on another mountain. Why then did I say yes when the teacher, Jim Pickering, asked if I would be interested in further excursions? Was it that I actually enjoyed battling against driving rain and gale-force winds, soaked to the bone by damp impenetrable mists: Had I derived some perverse pleasure from the wet peat which slurped around my boots, inside and out?

My interest in mountains grew with subsequent trips to the Lake District and, by the time I left school, I had climbed most of the major Lakeland peaks, ticking them off on lists at the back of my Poucher and Wainwright volumes. I had become the perfect example of a peak bagger. Eventually I returned to Wales and stood once again beneath the imposing Tryfan. Although some 500 foot lower than Snowdon, this was to be my first Welsh Three Thousander. All routes to the top are mercilessly steep and I forged up the north ridge with a sense of exhilaration and purpose. At the top I was rewarded with views as good as I have seen anywhere in the world.

That day I covered as many miles as I possibly could, seeking out every delightful corner of Glyder Fach, Glyder Fawr and Y Garn before descending the mystical Devil's Kitchen. I was spellbound - like a child let loose in a chocolate factory.

In the early eighties I became familiar with most of the Welsh Peaks, accompanying my uncle, John Gillham, on his research for "Snowdonia to the Gower", a 220 mile long distance route across Wales. It was in a discussion with John that I observed that little had been written for those who wanted to do the Welsh 3000's. "Write one", he said. I did not need much persuasion for the exploits of the likes of Joss Naylor and Colin Donnelly, those legends of the fell-running world, were always fascinating to me. I suppose Joss, who had also clocked unbelievable times on the Lakeland Fells and the Pennine Way, was an early hero of mine. It has to be said, however that I am a walker, although I have been known to pick up pace considerably to get down to the pub before closing time. I am indebted to Harvey Lloyd, for his

Roy Clayton

13

advice on the needs of fell-runners and for sharing with me some of his intimate knowledge of these mountains. Being the warden of the Pen y Pass Youth Hostel they are virtually in his back garden and he has many tales to tell. To say that I envy him is an understatement.

The Three Thousands route is twenty-seven miles in length and involves some thirteen thousand foot of ascent - a very serious expedition, especially in conditions less than ideal. It is an arduous undertaking over some of the most rugged mountains in British Isles. It is not a route for the inexperienced. for they may well be intimidated by some of the exposed ridges and steep descents.

The terrain is diverse. Snowdon's is one of magnificent crags and buttresses linked by razor-edged ridges. To the east of Y Garn, the Glyders are every bit as rugged - a chaotic assembly of boulder-ridden summits and craggy, lake-filled cwms. The Carneddau's wide, grassy plateaux are a delight to walk but can be confusing when the mist hangs low. Never is the need so great for a compass than on the Carneddau.

Some may feel that the twenty-seven miles is too great a task to be completed in one day and may wish to divide the walk into more manageable sections. Enjoyable ways to accomplish these are by youth hostelling or backpacking. The Youth Hostel Association has made many improvements over the years. They can now offer comfortable accommodation and a chance to socialise with people with similar interests. The hostels are listed in the data section at the back of the book. Backpacking offers a great flexibility of schedule - you can stop and pitch when you have had enough for there are many wonderful high-level wild campsites on all three mountain ranges in addition to the conveniently placed official valley sites. It must be stressed however that the route is only suitable for experienced backpackers. Steep descents and loose screes are infinitely more dangerous with the added encumbrance of a heavy rucksack.

I felt that it would be a good idea to include sections on

the Snowdon Horseshoe and also the Welsh One Thousand Metres Race. Both are classic routes in their own right and offer a different perspective to the mountains of the region.

It has been fifteen years since that first evocative journey over the Pennines and, in that time, I have never lost my feeling for mountain country. My renewed acquaintance with Snowdonia has reinforced my affinity and, although I have tramped the same ground many times, no two walks have ever been the same: the sun's rays, shadows cast by clouds, secretive mists and gleaming snows have all etched their different interpretations on the magnificent mountainscapes.

THE FIFTEEN PEAKS
Listed in order of altitude

Peak	height feet	height metres	range
Yr Wyddfa	3560	1085	Snowdon
Carnedd Ugain	3493	1065	Snowdon
Carnedd Llewelyn	3484	1064	Carneddau
Carnedd Dafydd	3426	1044	Carneddau
Glyder Fawr	3279	999	Glyders
Glyder Fach	3262	994	Glyders
Pen yr Ole Wen	3210	978	Carneddau
Foel Grach	3195	976	Carneddau
Yr Elen	3152	962	Carneddau
Y Garn	3104	947	Glyders
Foel Fras	3091	942	Carneddau
Garnedd Uchaf	3038	926	Carneddau
Elidir Fawr (Carnedd Elidir)	3029	924	Glyders
Crib Goch	3026	924	Snowdon
Tryfan	3010	915	Glyders

USING THE BOOK

John Gillham's panoramic drawings are great for getting the feel of the terrain and its 'ups and downs'. We would wish to emphasise however that they are not to scale and should be used only in conjunction with the Ordnance Survey Maps. (1;25000 Outdoor Leisure Maps are the best).

I have divided the Welsh 3000's route into three sections - Snowdon, the Glyders and the Carneddau and described it from Snowdon to Foel Fras (i.e. south to north). Route variations are described separately and I have added   very brief instructions for those who wish to do the journey from the North. All variations are shown on the map. As the 3000's starts on the summit of Yr Wyddfa (Snowdon) I have written brief descriptions of all the major ascents.

The data section at the rear of the book includes information on travel, campsites and youth hostels, cafés and inns. I have not listed individual accommodation as the information becomes so quickly out of date but the Tourist Board are very obliging and I have included their address and telephone number.

Harvey Lloyd's foreword gives invaluable hints for runners and advice on safety.

KEY TO MAPS

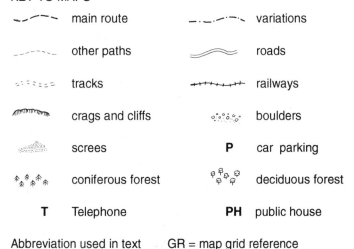

～～～～	main route	―.―.―¬.―	variations
_____	other paths	～～～	roads
⁛⁛⁛⁛	tracks	+++++++	railways
ᴍᴍᴍᴍ	crags and cliffs	₀°₀°₀°ᵤ°	boulders
⁙⁙⁙	screes	**P**	car parking
⫞⫞⫞⫞	coniferous forest	♧♧♧♧	deciduous forest
T	Telephone	**PH**	public house

Abbreviation used in text   GR = map grid reference

16

The WELSH THREE THOUSANDS

HISTORY & RECORDS
by Harvey Lloyd

Who it was who first donned his boots and set off for the summit of Yr Wyddfa with the intentions of traversing the Welsh three thousand foot peaks in one go is lost in the history of mountaineering. It would probably be in Victorian times, perhaps from a small hotel such as the Pen y Gwryd or Pen y Pass. It is recorded that Eustace Thomas of the Manchester-based Rucksack Club walked it in 1919 with a group of friends. His time, twenty-two and a half hours seems unremarkable enough but, considering he had passed his fiftieth birthday and had not taken up long distance walking until the previous year, it becomes more creditable. He had been described as an ageing business man with a weak digestion, troublesome feet and the beginnings of an elderly spread.

The walker of this time had none of today's high tech. gear. Heavy boots, tweeds, poor waterproofs and little equipment was balanced, however by a great enthusiasm for the hills and the challenge they issued. These men were true pioneers!

In the early days the route followed was nearly as variable as the times taken. Parties started from Nantgwynant, Llanberis, Pen-y-Gwryd and Aber. The idea of starting and finishing at the same place, making a round trip with no transport problems was soon adopted, the Llanberis or Ogwen Valleys being the main starting / finishing points. The Locked Book at the Pen y Gwryd Hotel is a mine of information on these early attempts. Many visitors to this hotel took on board the traverse of the Welsh 3's. They soon realised that there was "a record to be broken" in addition to the pleasure of a long day on the hills. Philips and Clay managed to fit in a hearty breakfast at the PYG and a forty minute tea-stop at Ogwen Cottage in a trip that took seventeen hours.

Herbert Carr, in 'The Mountains of Snowdonia', published in 1925, must have been instrumental in encouraging many of the early attempts. He wrote,

"Strong walkers will not visit Snowdonia many times without wishing to include the Carnedds, the Glyders and Snowdon in a single expedition. It is a very fine walk and, under favourable conditions, very well worth doing. In length it is about thirty miles when taken from Beddgelert, Conwy or Llanfairfechan. From thirteen to fourteen hours may be allowed, halts included, at an ordinary pace. It can be reduced by making the Ogwen Valley and Pen y Pass the points of departure and arrival. If part of the walk has to be done in the dark it is best to reserve the paths of Snowdon for the night watches. A moon, preferably full is to be desired."

Carr does not tell us if he attempted the walk himself but he was obviously writing to the 'hard men' of the twenties.

On the summit of Snowdon in Victorian times.

By the thirties the writer Showell Stiles had finished the route in twelve hours forty-four minutes and then Frank Shuttleworth achieved ten hours twenty-nine minutes.

Thomas Firbank set the scene for the post Second World War upsurge in interest. A fascinating account of his own record attempt is given in his book "I Bought a Mountain". He colourfully described the rigorous training he and his wife, Esme adopted for the event. They looked for ways to modify the route and came up with the idea of descending Crib Goch's north ridge thus saving valuable miles. In the Spring of 1938, the well publicised record attempt took place and the roadsides of Nant Peris were lined with spectators. On the summit of Snowdon the media were gathered in anticipation of a new record. The competitors were regally conveyed to the summit by a specially laid on train. Thomas Firbank did set the record along with companions W.E. Capel Cure and R.M. Hamer, reaching Foel Fras in a time of eight hours and twenty-five minutes. Esme, accompanied by Thomas Davies and hampered by a foot injury, limped home in an equally impressive time of nine hours twenty-nine minutes. Firbank prophesied that one day somebody would complete the journey in seven and a half hours but not much faster!

Firbank's successful attempt brought to the forefront the simmering controversy that had been around for sometime, "Should the mountaineer *run* in the mountains?" The attempt was frowned upon by the establishment and resulted in an apology by Firbank's companions being published in the Climbers' Club Journal for 1939. There was no doubt that it was not the done thing for members of the club to take part in such escapades that produce "some rather unwelcome publicity in the press".

After the war, more money, more leisure time and better transport facilities opened up Snowdonia to many more visitors. The fifties brought the athletes to the hills. John Disley set seven hours twenty-four minutes and Chris

Brasher and friends clocked six hours dead. The sixties saw Eric Beard home in the "impossible time of five hours thirteen minutes. Just before his untimely death in a car crash in 1969 "Beardie" had been on a training run with a friend, Joss Naylor whom he predicted would take his records. On a damp, misty June morning in 1973 the shepherd from Wasdale set off from the summit of Snowdon and four hours forty-six minutes later, still in mist, he touched the summit of Foel Fras.

The record was to stand until 1988 when Colin Donnelly, a member of the Eryri Harriers, recorded an unbelievable four hours nineteen minutes, including Garnedd Uchaf, a new summit added to the earlier list of fourteen by the latest Ordnance Survey maps. Colin was accompanied and paced by his team-mates from the Harriers.

The females too have left their mark with some very creditable times. Angela Carson ran 5 hours 28 minutes in 1989 to put herself in the record books. An event of this nature holds glory for all that take part. The group of schoolboys that completed it with Dr. G. Linsey Jones in 16 hrs 02 minutes must have been very pleased with themselves and one wonders how John Wagstaff felt in 1978 after completing the route three times in 22 hours 49 minutes.

Runner on the Crib Goch ridge

SPLIT TIMES

COLIN DONNELLY'S RECORD RUN - 11th June 1988

Sponsored by Reebock
Start time 10.30 am.

Peak	Split Time	Time from Start
SNOWDON		
Yr Wyddfa	0.00mins	0.00mins
Carnedd Ugain	4.56	4.56
Crib Goch	9.33	14.27
Blaen Nant	14.54	29.23
Nant Peris Post Office	7.32	36.50
THE GLYDERS		
Elidir Fawr	36.06	1hr13.00
Y Garn	22.00	1. 35.00
Glyder Fawr	19.00	1. 54.00
Glyder Fach	9.18	2 03.18
Tryfan	16.42	2 20.00
Ogwen	13.00	2 .33.00
THE CARNEDDAU		
Pen yr Ole Wen	38.00	3. 11.00
Carnedd Dafydd	11.00	3 .22.00
Yr Elen	20.00	3 .42.00
Carnedd Llewelyn	12.00	3 .54.00
Foel Grach	10.40	4 .04.40
Carnedd Uchaf	6.04	4. 10.44
Foel Fras	9.12	4. 19.56

Pacers - Don Williams, Emlyn Roberts, Del Davies, Huw Parry and Fon Williams

Angela Carson, running for the Eryri Harriers broke the womens' record with a time of 5 hrs 28.41 minutes.

ANGELA CARSON'S RECORD RUN - 5th August 1989

Sponsored by Reebock.

Peak	Split Time	Time from Start
SNOWDON		
Yr Wyddfa	0.00mins	0.00mins
Carnedd Ugain	5.25	5.25
Crib Goch	13.38	19.03
Nant Peris	35.13	54.16
THE GLYDERS		
Elidir Fawr	41.20	1hr35.36
Y Garn	26.58	2 .02.34
Glyder Fawr	23.11	2 .25.45
Glyder Fach	10.26	2. 36.11
Tryfan	24.19	3 00.30
Ogwen	23.42	3. 24.12
THE CARNEDDAU		
Pen yr Ole Wen	38.5	4 .03.02
Carnedd Dafydd	20.20	4 .23.22
Yr Elen	23.55	4 .47.17
Carnedd Llewelyn	13.0	5 .00.20
Foel Grach	12.48	5 .13.08
Carnedd Uchaf	6.23	5 .19.31
Foel Fras	9.10	5 .28.41

Time of day started - 10.30 am
Pacers Trefor Jones, Alan T Williams, David Carson and Tony Barker

THE WELSH THREE THOUSANDS ROUTE

THE SNOWDON GROUP

The Summits

Yr Wyddfa	**3560ft (1085metres)**
Carnedd Ugain	**3493ft (1065)***
Crib Goch	**3023ft (924)**

* incorrectly named Garnedd Ugain on the current O.S. Maps

Wales' mountains are firmly routed in its culture and heritage and none is greater than Snowdon, the Principality's highest summit and also the highest south of the Scottish Border. The Snowdon Group consists of five major peaks - Y Lliwedd, Yr Aran, Carnedd Ugain (sometimes incorrectly referred to as Crib y Ddysgl, which is the name of the ridge only), Crib Goch and Yr Wyddfa (the more acceptable Welsh name for Snowdon itself).

Yr Wyddfa, which means the tomb, has, in terms of mountain architecture, few peers within the United Kingdom. Its pointed summit is guarded by precipitous cliffs and, not surprisingly, affords the most spectacular panoramas in all Wales. These include the wide sweep of Cardigan Bay and the northern coastline. A dozen or so lakes and tarns of varying sizes are also in view. Dominant amongst these is Llyn Llydaw, which virtually fills the huge Cwm Dyli. Many people feel Snowdon has been spoilt by the construction of the railway and summit hotel (cafe). John Gillham wrote in his book 'Snowdonia to the Gower', "The flat-roofed monstrosity of Snowdon's 'hotel' and railway terminus is hated by all when closed but used by most when open." I certainly know I despised it when arriving hot and bothered ten minutes after closing time.

At Bwlch Moch with the Crib Goch Pinnacles towering above.

     The two feet seven inch gauge rack railway was opened in 1896 and had a tragic accident on the first day. On the descent a train was derailed and tumbled down the mountainside, narrowly missing several climbers. One person died - a passenger who leapt out of a moving carriage. The trains have since carried millions of joyful travellers to the rooftop of Wales. To some, including myself, it is comforting to see the plumes of smoke from the little steam engines, billowing from the high ridges or the sound of their hoots echoing through the clinging mists.

Crib Goch and its Pinnacles are probably the most exhilarating part of the Three Thousands. I vividly remember my first visit. The cloud base was barely over fifteen hundred feet and wispy grey mist swirled around my feet as I trod gingerly over the damp rock of the crest. It was an eerie experience and I could only imagine the drop through the clouds to the valley below.

Snowdon is steeped in history and legend. Echoes of the past reverberate around the ghostly relics of the old copper mines and quarries litter many routes to the top. Tales abound of King Arthur, who is said to have engaged in battle at Cwm Tregalan (south of the summit) with the treacherous Sir Modred. In the bloody battle Arthur forced his foe up the mountain to the pass between Yr Wyddfa and Y Lliwedd. Arthur was hit by an arrow but, before dying, it is said that he slew Sir Modred with the mighty sword, Excalibur. The place has been known since as Bwlch y Saethau (Pass of the Arrows).

Beneath Bwlch y Saethau is a "bottomless" lake, Glaslyn. Legend has it that in its depths lies a fearsome monster. Afanc, as it was called, originally lived in a deep pool, Llyn-yr-Afanc near Betws-y-Coed. He would often create havoc by causing floods in the neighbourhood. One day, after a particularly bad flood, the local inhabitants decided to act. They knew this beast had an eye for the ladies and lured him from the pool with a beautiful damsel. On his appearance, the unsuspecting monster was bound in chains by the men who had been hiding behind the bushes. He was then dragged across mountains and valleys before being dumped in Glaslyn. Some say he lives on deep in the lake! Other less romantic souls say he was just a beaver (well you know how these Welshmen exaggerate!)

SNOWDON 1 - YR WYDDFA to CRIB GOCH

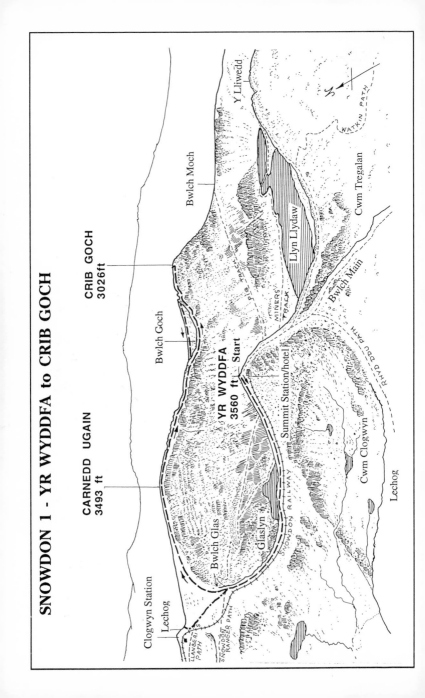

CARNEDD UGAIN
3493 ft

CRIB GOCH
3026 ft

Bwlch Moch

Y Lliwedd

WATKIN PATH

Bwlch Goch

CRIB GOCH 3026ft

PIG TRACK

MINERS' TRACK

Llyn Llydaw

Cwm Tregalan

YR WYDDFA
3560 ft   Start

Bwlch Main

Clogwyn Station

Lechog

Bwlch Glas

Glaslyn

SNOWDON RAILWAY

Summit Station/hotel

Cwm Clogwyn

RHYD DDU PATH

LLANBERIS PATH

SNOWDON RANGER PATH

Lechog

ROUTE DESCRIPTION

Yr Wyddfa (Snowdon) to Nant Peris
Distance 4 miles (6.5 kms)

After taking a last look from **Yr Wyddfa's** summit (always start at the trig. point), the marathon begins. A descent is made in a NNW direction, keeping to the path close to the edge of the huge corrie of Cwm Dyli and parallel to the line of the mountain railway. **Bwlch Glas,** the pass between Yr Wyddfa itself and Carnedd Ugain, is soon reached. The spot is marked by a huge obelisk and is the place where walkers using both the Miners' and Pig Tracks gain the ridge. The obelisk, although obtrusive, provides a useful aid when the winter snows lie deep. Before its construction, the upper regions of the Pig Track were uncertain and obscure in such conditions.

Beyond the obelisk, a sprawling cairn marks the departure of the popular Llanberis track. Our route veers slightly to the right, still keeping to the edge of Cwm Dyli. The wide, cairned track affords an easy pace as it climbs towards **Carnedd Ugain**, whose grassy top (3493 ft.) is crowned by a trig point. Although the views to Llanberis and the Glyders are striking, the gaze is firmly routed to the knife-edged ridge ahead, culminating at the Pinnacles of Crib Goch.

On descending Carnedd Ugain we are confronted by a choice of well-worn paths. This can be confusing in mist. It is advisable to maintain an easterly direction, close to the edge of Cwm Dyli, as this is where the path materialises when the ridge narrows. After dropping down into a hollow there is a magnificent view of Yr Wyddfa. The crest of the ridge is now followed before veering a few feet to the left of a rocky buttress. In favourable conditions the arete itself is the finest course as the climber is challenged to clamber over half a mile of rocky bluffs and clefts. The use of hands will be needed here. The course ceases to be obvious as the ridge

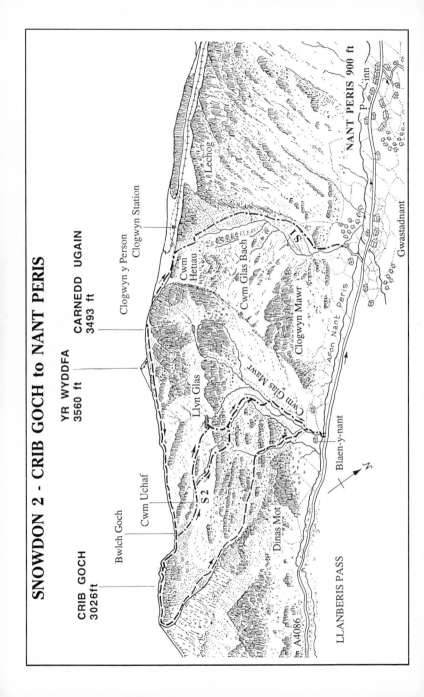

SNOWDON 2 - CRIB GOCH to NANT PERIS

CRIB GOCH
3026ft

YR WYDDFA
3560 ft

CARNEDD UGAIN
3493 ft

NANT PERIS 900 ft

P. inn

Gwastadnant

Clogwyn y Person

Clogwyn Station

Lechog

Bwlch Goch

Cwm Uchaf

S2

Llyn Glas

Cwm Hetiau

Cwm Glas Bach

Clogwyn Mawr

Afon Nant Peris

S

Cwm Glas Mawr

Dinas Mot

Blaen-y-nant

N

LLANBERIS PASS

A4086

appears to terminate abruptly at a cliff face. A path is available to the right however. It descends steeply some fifty feet by an assemblage of ledges to **Bwlch Goch** (marked Coch on current maps), a broader grassy pass containing a number of erosion control fences to the right of the path.

The lofty crests of the **Crib Goch Pinnacles**, which now lie ahead, form the most unassailable obstacle of the route. The most satisfying way is the one over the knife-edged crest although this is very exposed and not suitable for those with a nervous disposition. They should use the devious path, which circumvents the pinnacles on the Cwm Dyli side (right). The higher route commences ascent on the right hand side of the first pinnacle, where a steep path quickly attains the top and drops down the left side to the depression. The second pinnacle is tackled from the left side, passing a pile of stones, which marks the true summit (3026feet). This is exciting stuff - Snowdonia is laid beneath your feet. Teasing glimpses of Cwm Uchaf and Llyn Glas add to the drama of the situation. The final stage to **Crib Goch's** northern and more celebrated summit (3023ft) is the narrowest of all but, as with the Pinnacles, there is an easier route just below and to the right of the crest, which is used as a handrail. This second summit is recognised by a circular rock platform and a meeting of ridges.

Some walkers will descend Crib Goch eastwards, by way of Bwlch Moch, to their journey's end at Pen y Pass but the Welsh 3000's is barely started. Here the excitement continues on the arete, which curves northwards, encircling the rugged Cwm Uchaf and descending steeply towards the Pass of Llanberis*. All that we have gained on Snowdon is lost on the descent. Care needs to be exercised on this exposed spur. After half a mile of rapid descent, a precipitous scree path leads us westwards off the ridge, thus avoiding the vast cliffs of Dinas Mot. The scramble leads to a wet, grassy bowl, fringed by crags. Here the eastern banks of a stream (GR 622552), marked "falls" on the 1:25000 map, are followed *(water source)*. The track by the tumbling stream leads into **Cwm Glas Mawr** and beneath the huge rocky knoll of Dinas Mot.

After passing a sheepfold, a pleasant walk by stream-side pastures leads to the road at Blaen y Nant. The twisting narrow road is then followed for one and a half miles to the little village of **Nant Peris.**

* See Variation S1, which requires steps to be retraced along the Pinnacles to Bwlch Moch -for fast running times only.

The Snowdon Massif. From left to right the peaks are :-
- Y Lliwedd, Yr Wyddfa, Carnedd Ugain and Crib Goch

THE GLYDERS

The Summits

Glyder Fawr	**3279ft**	**(999Metres)**
Glyder Fach	**3262ft**	**(990)**
Y Garn	**3104ft**	**(947)**
Elidir Fawr*	**3029ft**	**(923)**
Tryfan	**3010ft**	**(915)**

* The more correct name for this mountain is Carnedd Elidir. Due to years of incorrect mapping it is seldom referred to as such.

From Capel Curig westwards stretches a 10 mile range of hard granite that has long been my favourite tramping ground. The Glyders or Glyderau, as they are sometimes called, include some of Wales most rugged peaks and issue a stern challenge for the hardiest walker. Five of our 3000 footers are located here. The Glyders' northern faces above Ogwen are bold, with deeply gauged cwms and magnificent sculpted cliffs and crags. Many of the lonely cwms contain delightful tarns.

Highest of the range, although only by a few feet, is Glyder Fawr, a rangy mountain with a large summit plateau of splintered rock and several jagged outcrops. The overall terrain is not unlike one would imagine the surface of the moon to be. Glyder Fawr's next door neighbour, Glyder Fach has even more spectacular features. Castell y Gwynt (Castle of the Winds) is a gaunt and massive serrated outcrop soaring from a sea of boulders. It forms a formidable obstruction to walkers from Glyder Fawr (most walk around its base). The Cantilever Slab, set slightly back from the summit, is a huge slab of rock, which seems precariously perched on an offset fulcrum. In fact it has been there for many thousands of years and has withstood the weight of the many travellers posing for their "all conquering "summit snapshots. Glyder Fach's most powerful feature has to be the Bristly Ridge. The jagged spur, which affords an excellent scramble, plummets to Bwlch Tryfan. This brings us to my favourite mountain, Tryfan, a magnificent wedge shaped peak, slightly out on a limb from the main ridge. It towers over Ogwen, proudly boasting its buttresses and gullies to all who venture on the A5 highway to Holyhead. Its sheer rock is impressive from every angle.

Standing on the shores of Llyn Ogwen, you cannot fail to be impressed by the bold facade of the mountain on the western skyline. Translated aptly as *The Eminence*, Y Garn certainly exudes nobility. It is strange to discover, however that it has a soft side, for once on the summit you can see its grassy southern slopes declining gently towards Nant Peris. In fact, with the exception of Esgair Felin, which towers above the bouldered gorge of the Pass of Llanberis, the southern slopes of all the Glyders are more gentle than their northern counterparts.

Elidir Fawr's (Carnedd Elidir) southern slopes have, in the vicinity of Llanberis, been scarred by the vast quarries of Dinorwig to reveal stepped terraces of bare rock surrounded by barren slag heaps. This conical hill, the most remote of the three thousands, withholds secrets, for it conceals the workings of a pump-storage power station. The 1680MW station, which is built into the mountainside by the shores of Llyn Peris, was opened in 1984 at a cost of £450 million. It was then the largest of its type in the world. At times of peak demand for electricity (i.e. at breakfast) water from the Marchllyn Mawr Reservoir is released through tunnels 2000 foot down to power the six turbines of the power station. At

The summit of Glyder Fawr looking to Tryfan & Glyder Fach

THE GLYDERS 1 - NANT PERIS to Y GARN

ELIDIR FAWR
(Carnedd Elidir)
3029 ft

Y GARN
3104 ft

GLYDER FAWR
3279 ft

quarries

Afon Dudodyn

inn **P**

NANT PERIS
900 ft

Dinas

Bwlch y Brecan

Foel Goch

Llyn-y-Cŵn

Esgair Felen

LLANBERIS PASS

to Pen-y-Pass

A4086

Gwastadnant

Blaen-y-nant

Afon Nant Peris

Main route via the north
ridge of Crib Goch

Variation S1 from Clogwyn Station
via Cwm Glas Bach

Variation S2 from Bwlch Coch via
Cwm Uchaf & Cwm Glas Mawr

times of low demand the turbines are reversed and water is pumped back up to Marchllyn Mawr, thus restoring levels, which can vary by over 150 feet.

ROUTE DESCRIPTION

Nant Peris to Idwal Cottage (Ogwen Valley)
Distance 9 miles (14.5 kms)

The next stage of the route leaves **Nant Peris** via a walled lane, sandwiched between the chapel and campsite and about twenty yards beyond the village Post Office. After about two hundred yards a footpath signpost points the way left along the narrow lane past the whitewashed cottage of Cerrig Dryddion (B & B) to Nant yr Fron, now a climbers' club hut. Just beyond the small cottage a stile to the right marks the start of the climb to Elidir Fawr. Here we strike uphill by a stone barn to a ladder stile in the top corner of the pasture. Beyond the stile the path continues through an iron gate, where a grassy track continues zigzagging uphill in delightful fields of bracken and foxgloves to reach a footbridge (GR 608596). Elidir Fawr lies directly ahead, its quarry-scarred, grassy facade soaring from the Afon Dudodyn *(water source)* to its craggy crest.

The path that has carried us thus far is abandoned, the bridge is crossed and we continue on a torturous slog northwards on a sketchy path climbing a crag-interspersed, grassy spur. After scaling a stile over a fence and an adjacent cross-wall it is best to rake across the grassy slopes towards the summit. Three erosion control fences have been erected in this vicinity but there are gaps quite close to the line of the old path. At about two thousand feet you can usually feel the breezes from the col ahead and soon the surrounding vista becomes more revealing. Across the deep and desolate hollow of the Afon Dudodyn, Foel Goch and Y Garn come into view with the fragmented crest of Esgair Felen plummeting

Looking towards Foel Goch, Bwlch y Brecan and Y Garn from Elidir Fawr

into the cleft of the Llanberis Pass.

A vigorous final assault on **Elidir Fawr** now begins over boulder-ridden slopes to its hard won summit. Decorated by a comforting wind shelter this is a fine place to dwell for those who are not racing against the clock. To the north west beyond, Marchllyn Bach and its craggy amphitheatre, lie Bangor and the Menai Straits, framed by a flat, chequered complex of pastureland, speckled with trees, houses and rivers. To the south all but the very top of Snowdon is shielded by the arm of Clogwyn.

Elidir's summit is left in a north-easterly direction in an initially rocky descent, aided by a few cairns. This soon transforms into a broad path on a grassy ridge, which, in turn, narrows into a rocky ridge with steep drops to the left. Marchllyn Mawr is framed beautifully from here - quite a spectacle if you are partial to nature being corrupted by symmetrical concrete shorelines. The route arcs round the massive grassy chasm of Cwm Dudodyn to Bwlch y Brecan, south of Mynydd Perfedd. Here we look down over the deep valley of Nant Ffrancon, which divides the Glyders from the Carneddau. The precipitous rugged slopes of Pen yr Ole Wen give a hint of the challenge yet to come.

THE GLYDERS 2 - Y GARN to the OGWEN VALLEY

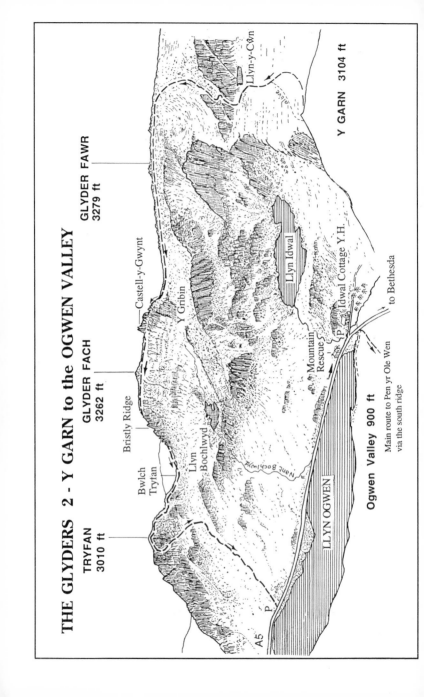

TRYFAN 3010 ft

GLYDER FACH 3262 ft

GLYDER FAWR 3279 ft

Y GARN 3104 ft

Castell-y-Gwynt

Y Gribin

Bristly Ridge

Bwlch Tryfan

Llyn Bochlwyd

Llyn-y-Cŵn

Llyn Idwal

Mountain Rescue

Idwal Cottage Y.H.

to Bethesda

P

Ogwen Valley 900 ft

Main route to Pen yr Ole Wen
via the south ridge

LLYN OGWEN

Nant Bochlwyd

A5

P

Only masochists will choose to ascend Foel Goch. Fine peak though it is, it fails to reach that magic three thousand foot figure and therefore mere mortals follow the low route, which circumvents it to the south. The ridge is rejoined above Cwm Cywion and this signals the challenge of **Y Garn.** A cairned track across loose slatey slopes leads to the summit, which boasts what I believe to be one of the finest views in Wales. The lakes of Llyn Peris, Ogwen, Bochlwyd, Idwal and Y Garn's own attendant tarn, Llyn Clyd are all visible, studded in a rugged mountainscape, which includes, the serrated tops and tremendous cliffs of Glyders Fawr and Fach. These are flanked by the distinctive profile of Tryfan.

From Y Garn there are initially two paths of descent towards Llyn y Cwn. One stays closer to the cliff edge. Both are usable and converge beyond a fence. As the path nears the desolate small tarn (Llyn y Cwn) the terrain becomes more boggy. Here we are joined by a path that has come up from Ogwen and the Devil's Kitchen. It is a good escape for the footsore and weary.

Passing the lake *(water source)* on the left bank, we round a rocky knoll before forging mercilessly upwards towards **Glyder Fawr.** There are several ways but the best one begins slightly to the left of a stony gully. The slippery, shaley path, which is extremely dangerous in wintry conditions, eases in the later stages as it zigzags to the barren plateau, eventually arriving at some jagged outcrops - a particularly large one marks the summit of our sixth three thousand footer.

The connecting path to Glyder Fach is a pleasant and entertaining stroll. The proliferation of cairns makes navigation easy in clear conditions but a little confusing in hill fog. The views down the Nameless Cwm to the left are breathtaking as a huge wall of rock, Clogwyn Du, plunges two thousand feet into a craggy abyss with Llyn Idwal basking in its rugged cwm far below. On the opposite side the heather-clad, stony southern slopes of Glyder Fach fall more gently to Llyn Cwmffynnon, Pen y Gwryd and Pen y Pass, which is hemmed in by the colossus of Snowdon.

At Bwlch y Ddwy Glyder we are confronted by **Castell y Gwynt** (Castle of the Winds), a juxtaposition of sharp rocks some two hundred foot in height. Practised scramblers can tackle them directly. It is easier however to pass to the right of them, although this does involve some loss of height and a slight scramble over bouldery slopes.

We are now on **Glyder Fach's** summit plateau: one, which again has been likened to a lunar landscape. The actual summit is formed by a massive jumble of boulders. Continuing eastwards we pass close to the Cantilever, a giant slab of granite precariously perched on a rock outcrop.

Bearing north-east from the Cantilever, a large obtrusion of rock indicates the top of the Bristly Ridge and forms a gateway to our eighth peak, Tryfan. Bristly Ridge itself is a time-consuming rock scramble and thus the best course is along the scree slopes to its right (east). They are steep and eroded and care should be taken, especially in snow or ice. This is spectacular stuff. Although Tryfan's triangular diadem, which now looms large before you, is not the highest of

Castell-y-Gwynt (Castle of the Winds), Glyder Fach. One of the summits many interesting features

38

The Bristly Ridge & Bwlch Tryfan, looking to Pen yr Ole Wen

the Glyder peaks, it ranks as one of the finest in Wales.

From the pass, **Bwlch Tryfan,** scale any of the half-dozen stiles across a dry-stone wall. Two possible routes to the summit now confront us. Both involve a certain amount of easy scrambling but the path closest to the wall, although providing more shelter, introduces it at an earlier stage.

The two pillars on **Tryfan's** diminutive but airy summit are known as Adam and Eve. In the true traditions of temptation many walkers are coaxed into jumping the gap between the two rocks. Little is achieved. One slip though and a lot could be lost so it's better to save your energies for the momentous journey ahead

The steep descent from Tryfan is the one used in a popular fell race, where speeds of under seven minutes have been recorded from summit to the shores of Ogwen. A course should be set northwards towards a secondary peak. On reaching the depression prior to this outpost, a left turn (west) is made down a steep scree gully. At the bottom of the gully the path heads NNW down steep grassy slopes with the crest of the north ridge well to the right. It meanders amongst

Adam and Eve, Tryfan's summit.

grass and crag to reach **Ogwen's** shores via a roadside car park.

If you intend to use the "fast" route up Pen yr Ole Wen's south ridge, a left turn is made along the road to Ogwen Cottage (Mountain Rescue Post) and Idwal Cottage Youth Hostel, where there are toilets, a refreshment kiosk and a car park. The opposite direction should be chosen for the more scenic east ridge. (See next chapter)

THE CARNEDDAU

The Summits

Carnedd Llewelyn	**3484ft**	**(1064 metres)**
Carnedd Dafydd	**3426ft**	**(1044)**
Pen yr Ole Wen	**3210ft**	**(978)**
Foel Grach	**3195ft**	**(976)**
Yr Elen	**3152ft**	**(962)**
Foel Fras	**3091ft**	**(942)**
Garnedd Uchaf	**3038ft**	**(926)**

If Wales is approached on the A55 coast road to Conwy, the ruffled edge of Tal-y-fan signals the beginning of the high Carneddau. This remote range of mountains rises from the sea, spreading southwards to the heart of Snowdonia. The Northern Carneddau consist of whaleback ridges and rounded hills, clad with pastel green tussocky grass, laced with boulders and dissected by clear, cool mountain streams. In the loftier southern peaks the rock surfaces more frequently in the form of cliffs such as Carnedd Dafydd's Ysgolion Duon (the Black Ladders) and Craig yr Ysfa. Both are much favoured by rock climbers. The tops are boulder strewn and interspersed with heather and bilberry. The last sentinel, Pen yr Ole Wen, watches over Ogwen where, in one foul swoop, craggy, scree-strewn slopes plummet over two thousand feet. Between north and south is an area as wild and remote as any in Snowdonia - one rather akin to the Cairngorms of Scotland.

The highlight of the Carneddau, provided that the weather is clement, will be the broad ridge from Pen yr Ole Wen to Foel Fras. Unfortunately route finding can be very difficult in misty conditions, especially in the region of Foel Grach. Judging by stories in the refuge shelter, many walkers have had narrow escapes from harsh conditions.

For the Welsh Three Thousander, passing the refuge hut should herald the start of a triumphant period, taking those

41

last steps in the fading evening light to the summit of Foel Fras.

THE ROUTE - Idwal Cottage to Foel Fras
Distance 9 miles (15 kms)

Eclipsing **Ogwen,** the precipitous fortress of Pen yr Ole Wen mocks the aching limbs, which have just surrendered over two thousand feet on a descent from the Glyders. In the space of just one mile all of that will have to be regained but take heart for, once you have cracked this one, the succeeding lofty Carneddau ridges will offer an easy-paced finale all the way to Foel Fras.

Just beyond the road bridge over the Afon Ogwen *(water source)* is a gap stile in the stone wall (GR 649606). After clambering over a series of rock "steps" to a grassy terrace, a fairly prominent track is encountered. It climbs steeply to higher slopes, which are clad with heather and bilberry. This subsequently gives way to loose scree and an unrelenting slog, which is nevertheless made bearable by stunning views across Ogwen to Tryfan's North ridge and Cwm Idwal. Snowdon appears over the top of the Devil's Kitchen.

Having been duped by a couple of false summits it is a relief to see the cairn and wind-shelter at the edge of **Pen yr Ole Wen's** large stony summit plateau. Now in northern vistas Carnedd Dafydd and Carnedd Llewelyn fill the frame with lesser peaks guiding the eye to Anglesey and the North Wales Coast. After climbing a little farther across the large, grassy plateau to the summit, a brief descent is made northwestwards to Bwlch yr Ole Wen. Here the delightful craggy arena of Cwm Lloer and its small tarn capture the attention. The path continues around the edge of the cwm before climbing north-eastwards on an undulating ridge to **Carnedd Dafydd**, whose summit also boasts a cairn and useful windshelter.

THE CARNEDDAU 1 - OGWEN VALLEY to CARNEDD LLEWELYN

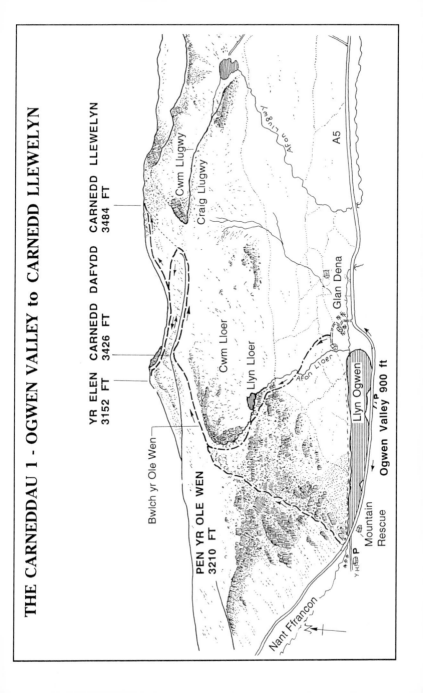

YR ELEN
3152 FT

CARNEDD DAFYDD
3426 FT

CARNEDD LLEWELYN
3484 FT

PEN YR OLE WEN
3210 FT

Bwlch yr Ole Wen

Cwm Lloer

Llyn Lloer

Cwm Llugwy

Craig Llugwy

Afon Llugwy

A5

Glan Dena

Afon Lloer

Llyn Ogwen

Ogwen Valley 900 ft

Mountain
Rescue

Nant Ffrancon

Y.H.

The track descending from Carnedd Dafydd hugs the edge of Ysgolion Duon (the Black Ladders). These precipitous cliffs at the head of the barren valley of the Afon Llafar are popular with rock climbers in the summer and snow and ice climbers in the winter. Although the massif of Carnedd Llewelyn (highest of the Carneddau but uninteresting from this vantage) lies ahead we will first visit the shapely peak of

Carnedd Llewelyn and the Black Ladders

Yr Elen to avoid scaling the former twice. This is done by contouring its southern slopes to the col above Cwm Caseg, where the pull to **Yr Elen** begins. En route you pass a spring *(water source)*. Being off the main ridge, this superb little peak is usually quiet. Carnedd Llewelyn now looks every bit a mountain, its rocky facade soaring above the shady depths of Cwm Caseg, whose diminutive tarn looks an idyllic wild campsite.

After returning to the col by way of a serrated rocky ridge, an attack is mounted on **Carnedd Llewelyn** on a good path at the edge of the cwm. It then veers to the right to attain the huge cairn and wind-shelter in the midst of a vast stone-

Carnedd Llewelyn seen from the connecting ridge to Yr Elen

THE CARNEDDAU 2 - CARNEDD LLEWELYN to FOEL FRAS

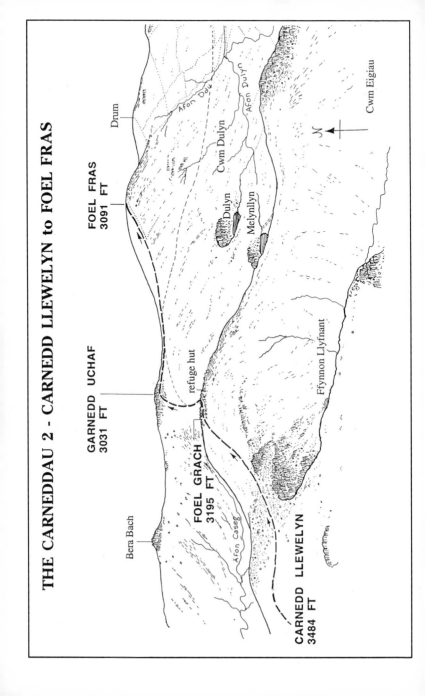

scattered, grassy summit plateau. Views have widened to encompass expansive stretches of the North Wales Coastline and the chequered emerald fields of the Conwy Valley, which lie beyond the sprawling grassy hills of the Northern Carneddau.

The ridge between Carnedd Llewelyn and Foel Fras is wide and, although pleasant to follow in clear weather, can be extremely confusing in mist. Good compass skills are essential here! A cairned track descends NNE before a slight rise to the bouldered summit of **Foel Grach.** Slightly to the north of the summit, camouflaged beneath crags, is the Refuge Shelter, much maligned by some, who feel it is alien to the wildness of the mountain environment. This view would almost certainly not be shared by the travellers who have gratefully stumbled across it in adverse conditions and

The ridge northwards from Carnedd Llewelyn to Foel Grach

have left messages of relief in the shelter's log book.

The twin lakes of Melynllyn and Dulyn lie tantalizingly out of view beneath Foel Grach's concave slopes and dark crags. A time-consuming detour would have to be made to see them. Most will want to press on to **Garnedd Uchaf** (the latest three thousander after surveying). Its stony top is gained with minimum effort. The terrain becomes increasingly less stony as the climb to our last peak, **Foel Fras** begins.

From GR 695677 a stone ridge-wall guides us to the summit trig. point. Somehow the dull top seems an unfitting climax to such a classic walk. However the solitude of this northern outpost allows a quiet contemplation of the day's triumphs.

ROUTES BACK TO CIVILIZATION

For those with friends with transport:

1) **To Bwlch Y Ddeufaen** (GR 721716)

Distance - 4 miles (6 kms)

Continue along the ridge (aided by ridge fence) over Drum (pronounced Drim), Carnedd y Ddelw and Drosgl to reach the Roman Road. Turn right to the terminus of the motor road half a mile distant.

2) **To lane beneath Penygadair** (GR 744694)

Distance - 4 miles (6 kms)

Continue along the ridge to intersection of fences (GR 704685) descend (trackless) by fence to meet right of way, which is then followed north eastwards beneath Pen y Castell and Penygadair to the road.

For the 'loners'

3) **To Aber**

Distance - 6 miles (10 kms)

A much longer walk. Follow the ridge to Drum where a rough vehicle track leads to the old Roman Road at GR 693722. Turn left along the old road, which becomes surfaced and follows the wooded lower valley of the Anafon to Bont Newydd before continuing to the village of Aber. (Coastal bus service.)

4) **To Rowen Youth Hostel** (GR 747721)

Distance - 5 miles (8 kms)

Follow route 1 for Bwlch y Ddeufaen and take the left fork in the lanes at GR 732715.

5) **To Gerlan/ Bethesda**

Distance - 5 miles (8 kms)

Re-trace steps back towards Garnedd Uchaf. Before reaching its summit, take the path which threads between this and Yr Aryg. A descent is then made on grassy slopes into Cwm Caseg, where a well-marked track leads to the head of the lane at GR 639665.

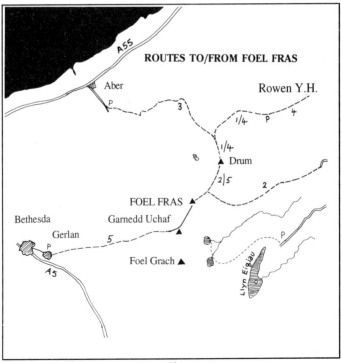

ROUTE VARIATIONS
THE WELSH THREE THOUSANDS

SNOWDON

VARIATION S1
FROM PEN-Y-PASS VIA CRIB GOCH-SeeMap Page 28

Although not accepted for record purposes, this route is probably the fastest of all. The Pig Track is followed to Bwlch y Moch but instead of following it into Cwm Dyli a bold attack is made on Crib Goch's steep, rocky flanks. The route is initially cairned but more often than not you can see walkers floundering at the foot of a crag. There are plenty of hand and footholds however and the difficulty is short-lived. The route continues on slatey slopes to Crib Goch's exposed top and from there to the summit of Yr Wyddfa is the reverse of the previously described 3000's route.

From Snowdon, the Llanberis Path is used initially on the descent but it is abandoned by the railway tunnel (GR 608561) near Clogwyn Station for a precipitous and spectacular descent into Cwm Glas Bach. Initially the route descends a series of grass "steps" before continuing along a rocky groove, raking left below the impressive cliffs of Llechog. The route now drops down a scree gully towards a stream. On reaching the stream *(water source)*, it deviates left to avoid rock ledges above the water's edge. From here the path becomes sketchy as it twists round crags and over steep, grassy slopes with a rocky spur to the left. The combination of short grass and an acute angle of descent make the terrain hereabouts very slippery after wet weather. Views across the valley to the Glyders are very impressive.

After going through a gap in a dry stone wall (GR 611570) head north-eastwards for some sheepfolds before veering left and passing the front of the Cwm Glas Bach Cottage, avoiding the house. Here an access lane* leads through a gate and over a bridge spanning the Afon Nant Peris to the road at Gwastadnant. A left turn is then made into Nant Peris, half a mile distant

* Please note that the lane is a negotiated courtesy route to the access area beneath Carnedd Ugain.

VARIATION S2

DESCENT OF CRIB GOCH BY THE RETURN TO BWLCH GOCH - See Map Page 28

Although this means retracing steps to Bwlch Goch, the pass between Crib Goch and Carnedd Ugain, the route can be marginally faster than the descent via the North Ridge. This variation was used by Colin Donnelly in his record run of 1988.

The key to this route is to boldly and directly descend the steep, scree-strewn flanks northwards into Cwm Uchaf. From Bwlch Goch, many try to contour the easier slopes to the left beneath Clogwyn y Person but consequently find themselves with crags and cliffs to negotiate. From the marshy bowl of Cwm Uchaf a continuation is made along the eastern banks of the stream *(water source),* which drains its tiny pools. The path, which varies between faint and non-existent, descends, threading through crags and bluffs into Cwm Glas Mawr, where the stream is forded. After traversing marshy grasslands and fording two more streams (GRs 618562 & 617563), a well defined stony path is joined. This descends close to the western banks of the main stream, passing the cottage of Blaen-y-nant before recrossing the stream via a wooden footbridge. After crossing another bridge, this time over the Afon Nant Peris, the road is met and followed to the left into Nant Peris.

N.B.
It is possible to vary the route from Cwm Uchaf by heading

NW over grassy flanks to Llyn Glas *(water source)*, a beautiful tarn set beneath the imposing cliffs of Clogwyn y Person. The eastern banks of the tarn are traced before turning right opposite its island. Soon after descending stony flanks a footpath becomes evident. It descends bouldery slopes close to the western banks of a stream (GR 619560). before joining the previously mentioned route beneath the cliffs in the marshy environs of Cwm Glas Mawr.

The S2 route of descent from Bwlch Goch to Llyn Glas

THE GLYDERS

There are few variations available on the Glyders. Experienced mountaineers (in no hurry and definitely not for those trying to do the route in a day) could scramble down Glyder Fach's Bristly Ridge then down Tryfan's spiky north ridge - better in ascent than descent. Another feasible possibility would be to retrace steps from the summit of Tryfan to Bwlch Tryfan and then take the path down to Llyn

Bochlwyd, one of the range's many delightful tarns. A well-used path continues down to Ogwen Cottage. Again this would add to the time taken.

THE CARNEDDAU

VARIATION C1
PEN YR OLE WEN via its EAST RIDGE-See Map Page 43

Although not quite as quick as the south ridge route, this delightful alternative is definitely for the connoisseur, offering fine views over Ffynnon Lloer.

The route begins at GR 668605, a short distance east of LLyn Ogwen. A public footpath points northwards on a gravel track which dissects a small fir plantation and passing, Glan Dena, the Midland Mountaineers Association's cottage. Just before reaching the farm, the track is abandoned for a path to the right which follows a wall northwards to a ladder stile. The stile is scaled and an intermittent path strikes northwards uphill by the Afon Lloer (*water source*). The stream is crossed at GR 668612 and the path continues over ground, which can be boggy after periods of heavy rain. The gradient steepens on approaching the intake wall (at the border of pastureland and mountainside) and a stile (GR 667617) by a gate is scaled. An indistinct path (ENE) now leads to the higher ground of the east ridge. A large crag appears to bar the way. Closer examination reveals a gully and an easy scramble up it gains the ridge. A delightful path continues along the ridge over heather and crag with a sudden view into the exquisite Cwm Lloer and its gem of a tarn. Views of the Glyders are highlighted by the wedge of Tryfan and Glyder Fawr, rent by the rugged defile of Devil's Kitchen, high on a rocky shelf above Cwm Idwal.

In the final stages the stony path hugs the edge of the cwm before leading westwards to the summit cairn on Pen yr Ole Wen, where the main route to Carnedd Dafydd is met.

THE 3000's NORTH TO SOUTH

Although the majority of walkers will start on Snowdon and end with the tranquillity of Foel Fras, many may prefer to tackle the route in reverse. The most obvious benefit from a north to south crossing is the fitting climax on the highest ground, Yr Wyddfa. If a fast time is combined with an early start you will be afforded the luxury of a pint at the summit hotel and the possibility of using the Snowdon Railway down to Llanberis. Another advantage would be that the descent from Snowdon to Llanberis is far safer in the fading light than the less frequented Carneddau tracks from Foel Fras.

Both itineraries have their individual appeals. The stiff climbs up Tryfan, Glyder Fach and Crib Goch's north ridge are far less intimidating in ascent than descent and that slog to Elidir Fawr from Nant Peris becomes a pleasant way down. Conversely the steep, scree-strewn descent from Pen yr Ole Wen to Ogwen becomes a real knee-trembler.

The fastest way to get to the summit of Foel Fras is to get transport to GR 721715 at the terminus of the Bwlch y Ddeufaen road, then climb Drosgl's north-eastern ridge to Drum and thence to Foel Fras. An alternative start is from the Bont Newydd Car Park at Aber (GR 662720). If somebody is giving you a lift they can take you to the end of the lane at GR 676714. Here a stony track is used to climb to Drum, turning right at the crossroads (GR 693722) between Garreg Fawr and Foel Ganol. Ignore the track to Llyn Anafon unless you fancy a steep climb out to the col between Drum and Foel Fras.

A swift pace can be adopted on the gentle Carneddau gradients but, in mist, route finding is difficult on the broad and featureless ridges, especially in the regions between Foel Fras and Garnedd Uchaf. Be careful not to be enticed on the short cut path from the pass between the two for this heads directly for Foel Grach, missing out the latter peak. As with the south to north route, Carnedd Llewelyn need only be scaled once. This is achieved by contouring its south western flanks after leaving Yr Elen. Carnedd Dafydd is gained with little difficulty, as is Pen yr Ole Wen. In descent, the east ridge is by far the most pleasant, although slightly slower than the more direct southern face. It also avoids those precipitous gradients and loose screes encountered throughout the descent to Ogwen.

The simplest way up Tryfan is the route described in the main itinerary, beginning from the car park at GR 658603. Although steep its course is never in doubt. An entertaining but time-consuming alternative would be to scramble up the craggy North Ridge route followed by Bristly Ridge to Glyder Fach. This suggestion is directed at experienced scramblers who will probably be taking two or more days to complete the excursion.

From Tryfan it's a clamber down to Bwlch Tryfan then up the screes to the east of Bristly Ridge to Glyder Fach, where the route continues over a chaotic boulder-strewn plateau to Castell y Gwynt. If you are familiar with the area you will be able to scramble directly down the rocky buttress but otherwise it would be prudent to detour to the left (this means losing a fair bit of height and still requires some boulder-hopping). It's a straight forward cairned path to Glyder Fawr, although the drop to Llyn y Cwn requires care, its shaly and friable surface makes the going difficult in places, especially in wintry conditions. From Llyn y Cwn the terrain is mainly grassy, except for the summit apex of Y Garn - one of the finest viewpoints in Snowdonia if you have time to stop

Foel Goch is the next summit in line but it is averted by a path which maintains a level course on its south-western slopes to reach Bwlch y Brecan. Here the assault on Elidir Fawr begins, contouring around Cwm Dudodyn before climbing a rocky spur which leads to this last Glyder summit.

After scrambling over boulders, an easy descent ensues over grassy slopes southwards to cross the Afon Dudodyn at a footbridge (GR 608596). The path then zigzags down fields, dappled with bracken and foxgloves, to reach a country lane by the cottage of Nant-y-Fron. This leads to the village of Nant Peris at the foot of Snowdon. Refreshments await at the Vaynol Arms.

We are now on the last leg but it is a real grind up the tarmac road to Blaen-y-nant Farm. Crib Goch just towers above - it's a veritable sting in the tail. The paths ascending Crib Goch from here are far less frequented than others on the Snowdon Range and present a stiff navigational test in the middle regions (where most peter out into sheep tracks). Initially the stony path from the cottage is good. It climbs by the rushing stream towards Cwm Glas Mawr but is left to cross the stream, aiming for a cleft in the craggy hillslopes to the left (GR 622562). Clamber up the left side of the falls, which cascade through the cleft then over a wide path on the steep red screes to Crib Goch's north ridge. From here its exposed ridges all the way - first to Crib Goch's summit thence over the Pinnacles to Bwlch Goch before the pull to Carnedd Ugain. Be careful not to be misled by paths which lead too far down the southern flanks above Glaslyn. From Carnedd Ugain's broad summit plateau it's plain sailing. If you've got this far the final slog following the path to the left of the Snowdon Railway will provide little resistance and there's always the thought of making it to the cafe before closing time!

SNOWDON - ROUTES of ASCENT

The main Welsh Three Thousands route, as is customary, is described from the summit. Many make the ascent by train but this is expensive and will not suit all pockets. I have therefore listed brief, "no frills" descriptions of the main routes to the summit. All are well used and should, in good conditions, be easily discernible underfoot.

ROUTE 1 - THE PIG TRACK

Distance	Three miles (5.1 kms)
Ascent	2400 feet (740m)
Start	Pen y Pass , GR 648557
Difficulty	Moderate.
Time	2-3 hrs up; 2 hours in descent

Sometimes incorrectly referred to as the Pyg Track after the Pen y Gwryd Hotel, this route actually takes its name from Bwlch y Moch (Pass of the Pigs).

It begins from the Pen y Pass through a gap in the wall at the top of the car park. A flagged path blasts its way through rocky outcrops above the Pass of Llanberis with the imposing peak of Crib Goch dominating views ahead. The path veers left to Bwlch Moch, where spectacular views of Cwm Dyli appear with the cliffs of Lliwedd soaring from Llyn Llydaw. The route now skirts the lower southern slopes of Crib Goch, climbing to a second higher cwm. Here the blue-green waters of Glaslyn lie cradled in the arms of Yr Wyddfa, Carnedd Ugain and the rocky spur of Y Gribin. From here the path continues over loose and fragile terrain to reach the infamous zigzags, a robustly constructed stairway, which climbs to Bwlch Glas, the pass between Yr Wyddfa and Carnedd Ugain. On reaching the obelisk at the pass, a left turn is made, tracing the cliff's edge parallel to the line of the Snowdon Railway to the summit.

The Ascents to Yr Wyddfa (Snowdon)

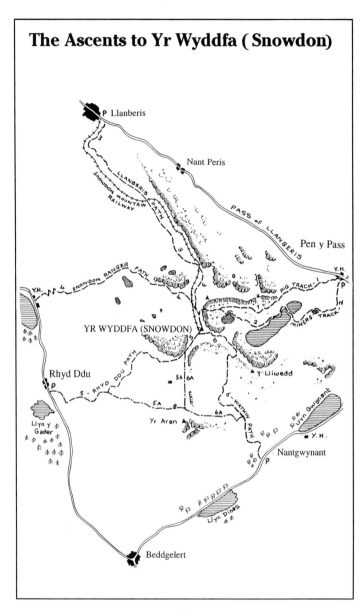

P Llanberis

Nant Peris

LLANBERIS PATH

SNOWDON MOUNTAIN RAILWAY

PASS of LLANBERIS

Pen y Pass

Y.H. P

Y.H. SNOWDON RANGER PATH

PIG TRACK

MINERS TRACK

YR WYDDFA (SNOWDON)

RHYD DDU PATH

Rhyd Ddu
P

5 RHYD DDU PATH

5A 6A

Y Lliwedd

5A

WATKIN PATH

6A

Llyn Gwynant

Llyn y Gader

Yr Aran

Y.H.

Nantgwynant
P

Llyn Dinas

Beddgelert

ROUTE 2 - THE MINERS' TRACK

Distance	three and a half miles (5.8 kms)
Ascent	2400 feet (740 m)
Start	Pen y Pass, GR 648557
Difficulty	very easy to Glaslyn then steep pull to the summit.
Time	2-3 hours up: 2 hours in descent.

This utilises part of an old Copper Miners' route connecting Bethesda with the Glaslyn Mine at the foot of Yr Wyddfa. The wide, stony track from the left hand side of the Pen y Pass Car Park is followed past Llyn Teyrn into Cwm Dyli. This vast hollow is filled by the expansive waters of Llyn Llydaw. The lake is crossed by way of a causeway and the stony track continues along its northern shores, passing the derelict crushing mill.

Beyond Llyn Llydaw the track climbs more steadily from the foot of Crib Goch to the shores of Glaslyn, a small tarn tightly enclosed by the mighty slopes of Yr Wyddfa and Carnedd Ugain and cradled by the rocky spur of Y Gribin. At the termination of the track, beyond the ruins of the old mine barracks, the gentle nature of the walk ceases and the collar work begins. A cairned path over loose, stony slopes leads to the Pig Track, which is now followed to the summit (see route 1).

ROUTE 3 - THE LLANBERIS PATH

Distance	5 miles (8 kms)
Ascent	3200 feet (980 m)
Start	Llanberis GR 583597
Difficulty	Easy but long. Can be hazardous in wintry conditions when snow and packed ice on the paths make it essential to be properly equipped with crampons and ice axe.
Time	3hours up: 2hours in descent.

Without doubt the easiest and most popular ascent of

Yr Wyddfa from the shores of Llyn Llydaw

Snowdon, the Llanberis path begins on a tarmac lane opposite the Royal Victoria Hotel. This climbs steeply before being abandoned for a signposted footpath to the left. The Snowdon Mountain Railway is never far away and provides a little interest on this relatively dull climb on the spur of Llechog, which rises from the valley of the Afon Arddu. Halfway House (GR 599569) provides refreshments in the Summer. Beyond Clogwyn Station the path cuts under the railway, revealing superb lofty views of the Pass of Llanberis. The route steepens as it veers southwards, traversing the shoulder of Carnedd Ugain to reach the monolith at Bwlch Glas (exquisite new views down Cwm Dyli), where it climbs the crest of the ridge, parallel and to the east of the railway track to the summit. Many people follow the course of the railway to the summit but this is ill-advised for reasons of safety. The path hereabouts is currently being improved.

ROUTE 4 - THE SNOWDON RANGER PATH

Distance	Three and a half miles
Ascent	3000 feet (925m)
Start	The Snowdon Ranger Youth Hostel, Betws Garmon, GR 565551
Difficulty	moderate
Time	2-3 hours up: 2 hours in descent.

This is probably the least used of the Snowdon routes and, although not the most spectacular, it does have its moments. It is also probably the safest route in the Winter months.

Zigzagging across rough, grassy slopes the path gives fine views towards Moel Hebog and the Nantlle Ridge, which lie invitingly across the sparkling waters of Llyn y Gader. As the path gains height the scene becomes more dramatic with Llyn Ffynnon-y-gwas nestling in the sullen, crag-ringed bowl of Cwm Clogwyn.

Once Bwlch Cwm Brwynog is reached the going gets

harder. The path now snakes up the rocky arm of Clogwyn Du'r Arddu. When the gradients ease, bear left to gain views of the cliffs of Clogwyn Du'r Arddu (a favoured spot for experienced climbers). It is now a simple ascent over the stony shoulder of Carnedd Ugain to reach the mountain railway, where a monolith marks the spot. Cross the railway and continue to Bwlch Glas. Here the path follows the crest of the ridge to the left (east) of the railway to Snowdon's summit.

ROUTE 5 - THE RHYD-DDU PATH

Distance	4 miles (6 kms)
Ascent	2950 feet (910m)
Start	Car Park (with toilets), Rhyd Ddu
	GR 571526
Difficulty	quite easy
Time	3 hours up: 2 hours in descent.

This interesting route begins on a quarry road to the north of the large car park. At GR 583525 the road, which heads for Bwlch Cwm y Llan between Yr Wyddfa and Yr Aran, is

At Snowdon's summit.

abandoned. A path to the left, beyond a gate, now wends its way amongst rocky outcrops to attain the Llechog ridge, where dark cliffs plummet in a spectacular scene to Cwm Clogwyn. A gravelly path snakes steeply uphill to Bwlch Main where you overlook the gigantic hollow of Cwm Tregalan towards the stony western flanks of Y Lliwedd. From Bwlch Main the path climbs steeply on a rocky ridge NNE passing the station/cafe en route to the summit.

Variation 5a via the South Ridge

.

At GR 583525 continue along the quarry road to Bwlch Cwm y Llan then head northwards on Yr Wyddfa's southern ridge to meet the Rhyd-Ddu route on Bwlch Main. (Advantage - less crowded although longer)

ROUTE 6 - THE WATKIN PATH

Distance	Four miles (6.4 kms)
Ascent	3400 feet (1045m)
Start	Lay-by car park, Pont Bethania, Nantgwynant, GR 628506
Difficulty	More ascent and tougher than other routes.
Time	3-4 hours up: 3 hours down.

The path takes its name from Sir Edward Watkin, a wealthy railway owner who engineered it as a donkey track. It was opened by Gladstone in 1892. The narrow tarmac northbound lane opposite the lay-by is followed until abandoned for a signposted path to the left, which winds into the beautiful glen of the Afon Llan. After passing some impressive waterfalls, the path climbs into Cwm y Llan dominated by the huge precipices of Craig Ddu, with the Snowdon massif forming the background. The stream is crossed by the ruins of Plas Cwm y Llan, once a quarry manager's house. On reaching the Gladstone Rock, the route veers westwards to circumvent Craig Ddu. It then climbs to the barren Cwm

Tregalan, which is hemmed in by the ramparts of Yr Wyddfa and Y Lliwedd. The ruined barracks and slag heaps of more slate quarries are passed. Here the Watkin path heads north-eastwards out of the cwm. In the upper reaches the path zigzags over the stony wilderness of Lliwedd's western flanks to reach Bwlch Ciliau, overlooking Cwm Dyli and its huge lake, Llyn Llydaw. There are fantastic views of Yr Wyddfa (L) together with the bold dark cliffs of Lliwedd (R) which flank the Crib Goch - Crib y Ddysgl ridge.

We have now joined the 'horseshoe' route. A wide path aims north-westwards for Bwlch y Saethau across a fairly level, airy ridge. Beyond the Bwlch, the ascent to Yr Wyddfa's summit is steep and care must be exercised. There are two paths - one heading directly along the edge for the summit and the other raking left to join the Rhyd-Ddu path on the South Ridge by a stone obelisk. Both climb over horribly loose, shaly slopes, which can be treacherous but the latter is marginally the easier course.

Variation 6a via Bwlch Cwm y Llan & the South Ridge

Turn left from the Watkin Path at GR 622520, just before it crosses the river, and climb to the old quarry tramway, which is followed to GR 617521. A path from here climbs to Bwlch Cwm y Llan, a pass between Yr Wyddfa and Yr Aran. Yr Wyddfa's south ridge is then followed to the summit. (Advantage - less crowded and avoids the Watkin Path's treacherous screes on the final pull to the summit. Still much ascent and quite arduous)

WELSH 1000 METRES RACE

After the Second World War the Welsh Fusiliers used the Welsh Three Thousands as a training exercise. Clad in full battle dress they competed against each other. Numbers grew and they were accused of contributing to the severe erosion on the mountainside and pressure was put on them to find an alternative. They chose the 'One Thousands', a route which visits the four Snowdonian Peaks which top one thousand metres in elevation - i.e. Yr Wyddfa and Carnedd Ugain from the Snowdon Group and Carnedds Llewelyn and Dafydd from the Carneddau.

THE ROUTE Aber to Snowdon

Distance: 22 miles (35.5 kms) -current route.
Ascent 8000 feet (2460 metres)
Checkpoints are numbered in brackets.

Shorter than the Welsh Three Thousands, this route begins on the seashore at Aber. It passes through the village and a wooded glen before skirting the top of Rhaeadr Fawr (Aber Falls), an impressive cascade. The route now enters the wild inner sanctum of the Carneddau via the remote hanging valley of the Afon Goch *(water source)*.

The main Carneddau ridge is joined between Foel Fras (left and Garnedd Uchaf (right). A well defined path is now followed over the rocky summits of Garnedd Uchaf and Foel Grach before continuing over **Carnedd Llewelyn(1)** and **Carnedd Dafydd(2).** Originally the descent was made directly from the latter peak down to Ogwen. Due to access problems this has been superseded by a more circuitous route, which heads eastwards to Craig Llugwy and down to the outlet of the **Ffynnon Llugwy Reservoir(3)***(water source)*. From here the reservoir approach road is followed to the A5 near **Helyg(4).**

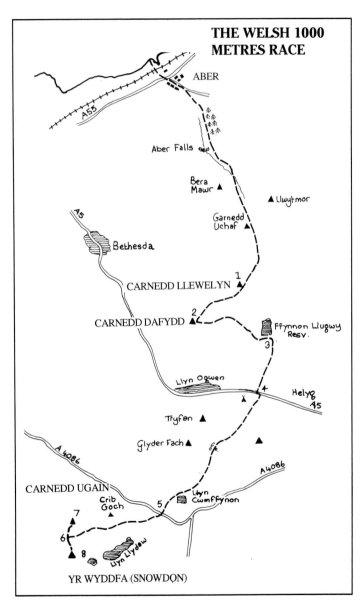

THE WELSH 1000
METRES RACE

ABER

A55

Aber Falls

Bera
Mawr ▲

▲ Llwytmor

A5

Garnedd
Uchaf ▲

Bethesda

1
CARNEDD LLEWELYN ▲

2
CARNEDD DAFYDD ▲

Ffynnon Llugwy
Resv.

3

Llyn Ogwen

Helyg
A5

Tryfan ▲

Glyder Fach ▲

▲

A4086

A4086

CARNEDD UGAIN

Crib
Goch ▲

5

Llyn
Cwmffynon

7

6

8 ▲

Llyn Llydaw

YR WYDDFA (SNOWDON)

*Tryfan seen from Gwern y Gof Isaf Farm's campsite, nr Helyg
with Glyder Fawr on the horizon to the left.*

After crossing the busy road the route continues up the desolate cwm of Nant yr Ogof *(water source)*, climbing to gain
the Glyder Ridge at Llyn y Caseg-ffraith. The old Miners'
Path is joined here. It traverses the grassy saddle between
Glyder Fach and Foel Goch before descending craggy slopes
towards Pen-y-Gwryd. The cascading stream, passed on the
descent, is a *water source*. The path is left at the wall crossing and a bee-line is made westwards for Llyn Cwmffynon
and then **Pen y Pass (5)**.

     The Pig Track must then be followed into Cwm Dyli
before climbing the zigzags *(water source)* to **Bwlch Glas
(6)** and heading north-eastwards to **Carnedd Ugain (7)**.
Steps are then retraced to the col before that final climb by
the railway track to **Yr Wyddfa (8)**.

Steps are then retraced to the col before that final climb by the railway track to **Yr Wyddfa (8).**

HISTORY

In 1971 the inaugural Welsh 1000 Metres Peak Race took place and had nineteen entrants. The fell runners' class was won by Dennis Weir in three hours forty-seven minutes, two minutes outside Ted Norrish's unofficial 1970 record. The following year Joss Naylor won in three hours thirty-seven minutes. Joss was to win the race for five consecutive years, clocking up a best time of 3hrs 37mins. Mike Short broke Naylor's record by forty-five seconds in 1978 .

Access problems then required the course to be re-routed as mentioned above (1979). Mike Short won the race in 3.32.59 and dominated the event into the eighties (five consecutive victories). The last two races have been won by Colin Donnelly, although Mike Short's records still stand.

The womens' record is held by Carolyn Hunter Davies in a time of 4.30.53.

There are currently four classes in the race:-

A   Fell Runners

B   Mountaineers wearing boots and carrying/
wearing specified items of equipment.

C   As B but starting from Ogwen.

D   As B but for service teams.

There are prizes for men, women, veterans and super-veterans and declared teams.

The race has recently been re-named "The Snowdonia Summits Marathon" and is organized jointly by the Gorphwysfa Mountaineering Club and the Army in Wales. It is always held on the first Saturday in June.
See address in the data section for entries.

The SNOWDON HORSESHOE

Distance   8 miles
Time 8 hours

The Snowdon horseshoe has been described as one of the finest ridge walks in Europe. It does indeed take the description "ridge" to the limit. Tracks in some places become non existent as the foot-moulded razor-edged crests plummet to the valleys, leaving the walker exposed and at the mercy of the elements. It is all exhilarating stuff and adds to the excitement of this great walk.

Most people start the walk from Pen y Pass Youth Hostel and make for Crib Goch on the Pig Track but I think that to do it in the reverse order is best. Firstly the loose upper sections of the Watkin Path are much better in ascent and secondly, I think the prospects from the Crib Goch - Crib- y- ddysgl Ridge are better in this direction.

The eight foot wide Miners' Track from the left hand side of the car park (GR 648557) heads in a southerly direction. A good pace can be maintained over the path which gains little height at first.

After a quarter of a mile the track veers to the right, exposing the sheer cliffs of Y Lliwedd and, in the mid-distance, the conical peak of Y Wyddfa. To the right and looking equally magnificent are the quartz-banded ramparts of Crib Goch. The path continues past the old derelict copper-mining cottages which overlook Llyn Teyrn, a small tarn, secretly set in a grassy hollow amongst small bluffs. It then climbs out of the hollow to a corrugated iron shed on the shores of Llyn Llydaw, a much larger lake which occupies the vast chasm of Cwm Dyli. Here we leave the old Miners' Track which blasts a course up Cwm Dyli. Our route bears left along the southern shores of Llyn Llydaw and crosses a metal footbridge to reach a stretch of fencing, erected to control erosion. We now strike uphill at a moderate gradient. A

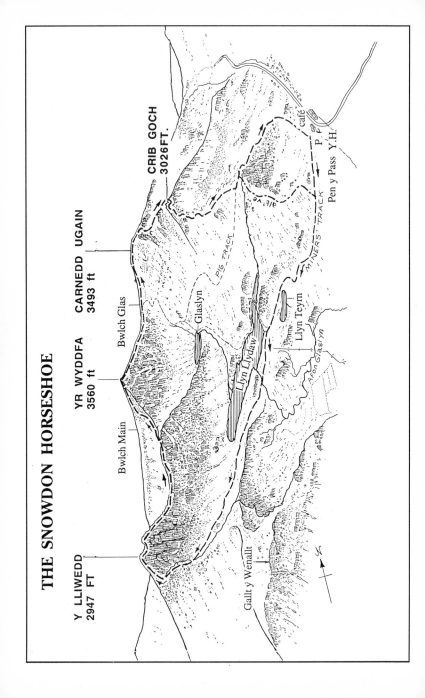

THE SNOWDON HORSESHOE

Y LLIWEDD
2947 FT

YR WYDDFA
3560 ft

CARNEDD UGAIN
3493 ft

CRIB GOCH
3026FT.

Bwlch Main

Bwlch Glas

Glaslyn

PIG TRACK

Llyn Llydaw

Llyn Teyrn

MINERS TRACK

Afon Glaslyn

Gallt y Wenallt

café

Pen y Pass Y.H.

P.P.

twenty foot dip then precedes an area of slightly boggy flat ground, which offers brief respite before the real collar work commences on an arduous ascent towards Lliwedd. Height is gained rapidly as the stony track weaves around a series of rock ledges to attain the ridge by a large cairn (GR 631535) to the north east of Lliwedd Bach. Although the majestic mountain scenery of Snowdon and its satellites dominates, it is pleasing to see the contrasting softer scenery contained in the wide sweep of Nantgwynant to the south. Its shimmering lakes and pastures are patched with woodland and fringed with the gritty knolls of the Moelwyn-Siabod ridge.

The route now continues along the cliff-edge to Lliwedd Bach. This will be remembered for its secret niches proffering magnificent views of the majestic dark precipices of both East and West Lliwedd, which tower 1000 feet above Llyn Llydaw, now far below us. The bouldery cairned path keeps close to the edge before gaining both the Lliwedd summits. From the top of the west summit Glaslyn peers over the rocky spur of Y Gribin.

A descent is now made on heavily bouldered slopes to Bwlch Ciliau, where we are joined by the popular but badly eroded Watkin Path to Y Wyddfa's summit. Continuing along the ridge to Bwlch y Saethau (Pass of the Arrows) there is a wonderful retrospective view down the length of Cwm Dyli, taking in Crib y Ddysgl, Crib Goch and the latter part of the 'horseshoe'.

Now the Snowdon summit massif lies ahead. There is a confusing network of paths in this vicinity, including one that descends the spur of Y Gribin and some that just visit the edge above Glaslyn. In mist it is best to stick to the main route which now keeps below the crest of the ridge overlooking the vast hollow of Cwm Tregalan. The final stages of the route to Y Wyddfa's summit can be tricky for its flanks are steep and the shaley surface rock friable. Two paths exist. The one to the right aims boldly for the summit but is not recommended. The one to be used slants to the left across the slippery southern slopes. It climbs steeply, twisting and turning in an impossible task to find an easy way but, finally, it attains the southern ridge by a huge monolith. Here the Beddgelert Path is joined. Looking westwards the impressive peaks of the Nantlle Ridge and Mynydd Mawr are added to the view beyond Rhyd Ddu and the nearby lakes of Cwellyn, Gadair and Dywarchen.

It is now just a short easy climb on to Yr Wyddfa's summit, passing the cafe en route. The summit cairn is usually swarming with tourists, many of whom have made the journey on the mountain railway. They will share with you one of the great panoramas of Europe. Although not of alpine proportions, the view from Snowdon reveals magnificent glacial architecture in an intricate labyrinth of cwms, aretes and buttresses. In good conditions much of Wales can be seen - its coastline, distant towns and range upon range of mountains paling to the blue horizon.

The route from the summit to Crib Goch is identical to that described in the Welsh 3000's. Briefly, it descends to Bwlch Glas close to Cwm Dyli's edge and parallel to the railway before the easy climb to Carnedd Ugain. From here the crest of the ridge is followed on a tricky course over Crib y Ddysgl to Bwlch Goch before the final airy assault on Crib Goch and its infamous 'Pinnacles'.

The descent from Crib Goch can be tricky, especially when wet. It begins with an airy passage over shaley slopes eastwards towards Bwlch Moch. This terrain ends abruptly at a rocky ledge, where good hand and footholds help the walker down to a cairned track, which then winds more sedately down the steep lower slopes to meet the Pig Track at Bwlch Moch. The newly renovated track is somewhat overdone and unsympathetic to its surroundings. To be fair time and a million boots will blend it in and it does offer a quick way back to base at Pen y Pass. It also has good views of the harsh boulder-strewn Pass of Llanberis and the rocky crest of Esgair Felen.

DATA SECTION

MAPS

You can get by with the Landranger 1:50000 No 115 "Snowdon & Surrounding Area" but the latest double sided Outdoor Leisure 1:25000 No.17 "Snowdonia: Snowdon & the Conwy Valley Areas" is far superior for route finding as it shows fences, walls and details many more of the crags.

O.S. Pathfinders SH65/75 plus SH66/76 (1:25000) cover the route but not the return to Aber.

TRANSPORT

BY RAILWAY

1 North Wales Coastal line via Llandudno calls at Bangor. Link from Llandudno Junction to Conwy Valley Stations of Tal-y-cafn, Llanrwst and Betws-y-Coed.

2 Porthmadog via rail from Shrewsbury via Machynlleth

BY BUS

Local Bus timetables including the very useful Snowdon Sherpas Service can be obtained from :-

National Park Office,	
Penrhyndeudraeth,	
Gwynedd LL48 6LS	Tel. 0766 770274
or	
County Planning Officer,	
Gwynedd County Council,	
County Offices,	
Caernarfon,	
Gwynedd LL55 1SH	Tel 0286 672255

Please enclose a 9" x 6" s.a.e.

ACCOMMODATION

YOUTH HOSTELS

Pen-y-Pass,
Nantgwynant,
Caernarfon,
Gwynedd LL55 4NY
Tel. 0286 870428

Harvey's place and the best situated for a south to north attempt.

GR 647557

Llanberis,
Llwyn Celyn,
Llanberis,
Gwynedd LL55 4SR
Tel. 0286 870280

Good for those who intend to get to Snowdon via the mountain railway.

GR 574596

Snowdon Ranger,
Rhyd Ddu,
Caernarfon,
Gwynedd LL54 7Y
Tel 0286 650391

Well placed for those who want a quiet ascent of Snowdon (ie the Snowdon Ranger Path)

GR 565550

Bryn Gwynant,
Nantgwynant,
Caernarfon,
Gwynedd LL55 4NP
Tel. 076686 251

Ideally placed for those wanting to climb Snowdon via the Watkin path.

GR 640513

Idwal Cottage,
Nant Ffrancon,
Bethesda,Bangor,
Gwynedd LL57 3LZ
Tel. 0248 600225

In the Ogwen Valley. Well placed for those taking more than one day for the route.

GR 648604

Rowen,
Rhiw Farm,
Rowen, Nr Conwy.

Close to the end of the walk in the Northern Carneddau.
GR 747721

Closed in Winter & limited opening in the summer months.
Enquiries to Wales Regional Office Tel 0222 231370 or
0492 530627

Youth Hostel Association National Office
Trevelyan House,
8, St Stephen's Hill,
St. Albans,
Herts AL1 2DY   *for membership details*

HOTELS

Many at Capel Curig, Betws y Coed, Beddgelert, Bangor and Caernarfon. Details can be obtained from the Tourist Information Centre, Oriel Pendeitsh, Caernarfon, Gwynedd LL55 2PB. Tel 0286 672232.

CAMP SITES

Nant Peris GR 604587 (not marked on current map),
LLanberis GR 563633,
Beddgelert GR 577491,
Betws y Garmon GR 536575 & 546567,
Gwern Gof Isaf GR 686601
Gwern Gof Uchaf GR 673603 (not marked on current maps),
Capel Curig GR 743572,
Dwygyfylchi GR 730770.

CAFES

Pete's Eats, Llanberis - has been described as the best café in the world.
Pinnacle Café, Capel Curig.
Gorphwysfa Café, Pen y Pass
Snowdon View Café, Capel Curig

GOOD PUBS

Cobdens, Capel Curig - climbers' bar built into a rockface at the rear of the building.Bar meals and accommodation available
Bryn Twrch, Capel Curig - pleasant accommodation available.

Ty'n y Coed, Capel Curig - bustling pub. Bar meals and accommodation available.

Vaynol Arms, Nant Peris - Bar meals and accommodation available.

Royal Victoria, LLanberis.

Padarn Lake Hotel, Llanberis.

Royal Oak Hotel, Betws-y-Coed. - good bar at the car park end. Bar meals and accommodation available

Pen-y-Gwryd Hotel, Nantgwynant - good atmosphere. Accommodation available.

Cwellyn Arms, Rhyd Ddu, Good bar meals

The Heights Hotel, Llanberis, For BMC Members. Has a climbing wall in the back bar. B & B and bunkhouse type accommodation.

SOME USEFUL ADDRESSES

FELL RUNNERS ASSOCIATION
    M.J. Rose,
    15, New Park View,
    Farsley,
    Pudsey
    Leeds
    West Yorks LS28 5TZ

ONE THOUSAND METRES RACE
    (run 1st Saturday in June)

    C. Middleton,
    31, Cherry Tree Avenue,
    Kirby Muxloe,
    Leicestershire

LONG DISTANCE WALKERS' ASSOCIATION
    MEMBERSHIP SECRETARY
    Kevin Uzzell,
    7, Ford Drive,
    Yarnfield,
    Stone
    Staffordshire. ST15 ORP

GLOSSARY OF WELSH WORDS

Aber	river mouth
Afon	river
Arddu	black crag
Bach/fach	small
Bedd	grave
Betws	chapel
Blaen	head of valley
Bont/pont	bridge
Bwlch	pass
bws	bus
Cae	field
Caer	fort
Carnedd/Garnedd	cairn
Capel	chapel
Carreg/garreg	stone
Castell	castle
Cefn	ridge
Cors/gors	bog
Clogwyn	cliff
Coch/goch	red
Coed	wood
Craig	crag
Crib	sharp ridge
Cwm	coomb
Cwn	dog
Dinas	hill fort(or town)
Diolch	thank you
Du/ddu	black
Drum/trum	ridge
Drws	door
Dyffryn	valley
Dwr	water
Eglwys	church
Esgair	ridge
Eryri	eagles abode
Fawr/mawr	large
Felin/melin	mill
Ffordd	road
Ffynnon	spring
Ffridd	enclosed grazing land
Glas/las	blue, green
Gwyn	white
Gwynt	wind
Hafod	summer dwelling

77

Hendre	winter dwelling
Isaf	lower
LLan	church or blessed place
Llwybr Cyhoeddus	public footpath
Llwyd	grey
Llyn	lake
Maen	stone
Maes	field/meadow
Moch	pig
Moel	featureless hill
Mynydd	mountain
Nant	stream
Ogof	cave
Pant	clearing, hollow
Pen	peak
Person	cascade
Plas	mansion
Pwll	pool
Rhaeadr	waterfall
Rhyd	ford
Saeth(au)	arrow(s)
Troed	foot of
Twll	cavern
Ty	house
Uchaf	high, higher
Waun	moor
Wen	white
Wrach	witch
Ynys	island
Y, Yr	the
Ynys	Island

BIBLIOGRAPHY

The Welsh Peaks - Poucher   (Constable)
Guide to Wales' 3000 Foot Mountains   H. Mullholland (Mulholland Wirral)
The Ridges of Snowdonia - Steve Ashton (Cicerone)
Snowdonia to the Gower - John Gillham (Diadem)
Hillwalking in Snowdonia- E.G. Rowland (Cicerone)
Hillwalking in Wales Vols 1 & 2 Peter Herman (Cicerone)
The Mountains of Wales - Terry Marsh (Hodder)
I Bought a Mountain - Thomas Firbank (Harrap)
Wild Wales - George Borrow (Fontana)

Heading towards Foel Grach from GarneddUchaf with Carnedd Llewelyn and Yr Elen in the Background.

NOTES

....
....
....
....
....
....
....
....
....
....
....
....
....
....
....
....